37/83

37/83

A book of poetry

MARCO A. SOTO

SPRING CEDARS

Copyright © 2022 by Marco A. Soto

All rights reserved.

First edition, 2022

Cover photo by Marco A. Soto

Book design by Spring Cedars

ISBN 978-1-950484-33-1 (paperback)
ISBN 978-1-950484-34-8 (hardback)
ISBN 978-1-950484-35-5 (ebook)

Published by Spring Cedars
Denver, Colorado
info@springcedars.com

TABLE OF CONTENTS

An Innocent Smile Among a Million Trees 9
First House 10
Jump, Breathe, and Close your Eyes 12
Backseat: Otherwise 13
Five Minutes Ago 14
We Are 15
Growing Ill 16
Tafamo 17
Where Will You Be 18
In Hopes of One Day Left 19
Rush; Deep Impact 20
Six Hours Apart 21
Not True, But First 22
To the Lost 24
Alive: I 25
Poor Man's Choice 26
Jack of all Trades 27
On a Void 28
Hundred Percent 29
Half Life 30
Alive: II 31
Ashes Left Behind 32
Bad Thoughts 34
Emasculation: Through Kind Words 35
The Fall Around Me 36

Cold Patch	37
In the Contrasts	38
Step on the Stones Above the Water	39
Layers	40
A Day of Do and Do	41
Shrug to Kismet	42
Fill Less	44
Snaketh	45
At Odds	46
In Sight, yet not Always in Mind	47
This is and That is, More	48
Struck Luck: 15	50
Such Depth of your Smile	51
Failure: the Absence of Success	52
Day In, Day Out	53
Shoulder on Hand	54
Touch	55
Facing Capsize	56
Sweet Words	57
Mariana Eyes	58
A Lone Stride to Fall	59
Unequivocal Love	60
Beautiful Star Dust	61
Double Sunrise	62
A Certain Hour	63
Genuine Care	64
Nothing, is Okay	65

Antigua in Pax (la receta) 66
An Intuitive Existence in the Rest of the World 67
I Almost Gave Up 68
As if 70
One Face Coin 71
Finding You Within a Mirror 72
Irreplaceable 73
Accent 74
Another Drop of Rum 75
Truck or Van 76
Ever so Bright 78
Feeling in Silence 79
Doubtless: Preamble to a Story 80
Amongst All 82

This book is the result of a
roller coaster of heartaches, joys, and sorrows.
"When the going gets tough, the tough gets going."

Dedicated to all who have been
by my side through the ups and downs of life.
Those that are, that have been, and that couldn't be.

An Innocent Smile Among a Million Trees

In a rearview mirror, a city, its people and politics
Unable to see much, too many cars
A single thought, momentary messages from afar
The path narrows around every winding turn

Radiantly, a burning star hides behind the horizon
Painting the day with a spatter of stars and darkness
A number of crossroads, I rather use the dirt path
Serenity and unequivocal love stand out in the night

Two contrasting hands hold steady the love of relatives
Winds whistle a priceless melody, the mist is coming in
Cascades and frogs chant along, connected at the heart
Give all the innocent a smile, thank nature and the
elements

First House

So far apart and distant
And ceilings seemed so tall
An impermeable feeling
Protecting me from all

That minute bed on a corner
An armoire with a mirror
Eclectic shirts and pants
A few pairs of shoes, just enough

A window, a glass block
Some daylight shining through
That poorly placed door
Letting in nightly whistling drafts

That constant heavy rain
Pooling at the top
Droplets falling inside
Loud as they hit the ground

Next door the secret room
Where my brother lay his head
Not much older than me
But such different worlds

Those narrow stairs going up
Yellow slick floor, fresh smell
Gallop through my sister's room
To a balcony, to view life

Malleable while young
Not yet suffering life maladies
With most of the world unknown
On the place that was my house.

Jump, Breathe, and Close your Eyes

Do not be disturbed, or perhaps just scared
This beautiful life is better shared

My brown and your green eyes
Stare blankly into the blue-lit skies

I cannot pay for how I smile when you're near
I just encountered you and this soon you are so dear

The candid yet timid smirk that paints your face
There are never enough words to describe such grace

With your fingers, write on the blue sky, add that smile
While the pleading flowers say "will you stay a while?"

I've not known such good fortune, with you included
The life I was dealt was simple, yet secluded

Thanks for coinciding with me, in such a unique place
Imagining what to say, but silence is best in this case

Backseat: Otherwise

Restless, night chills
Conversations, with old
With new, none flirtatious
Talkative, assertive at times
Anxious and rattled
Shaken to the core
Gone before sunrise
Thinking while alone
Sitting and laying
A hat for a pillow
While the road winds
The blankets above
Insulate and hide sun rays
The hours pass by
As if flying home
Tool, bleed into my ears
Rest finally rest.

Five Minutes Ago

You left, never looking back
Not thinking, just being
Across night slow, driven

With a temper of tempest
As if walking out in anger
For no one reason alone

In furor and scarlet eyes
Through linear dark skies
Not a sound, not a breath

Here, standing still, alone
Sensing those minutes
Calmness behind you

They and we all turn to you
In fear and in thanks
As those minutes are warm

We Are

One long time ago, perhaps not so long.
We come in screams and tears.
On top of that chain, a necessary evil.
The first sounds create a concoction of emotions.

Not a trace of memory, not from the beginning.
We begin again at the end.
Each speck of dust will again die to be free.
A life sentence for each, no trial, no judge.

All that was, is, and will be, all will stop.
Time, look at a clock, and see each second die.
All the Gods to praise, with so many names, believe.
Those memories, light years away, and fading.

This never ending, never stopping place called home.
As a phenomenon that we foresee, it is inescapable.
On that first day, a number is drawn, live and wait.
Then, the unifier calls that number, time to go.

Growing Ill

Those, who say they can, and don't
The ones that were, but aren't, and still linger
Being told yes, while a physical answer is absent
That ever present complex, not everyone is equal

Be tender to one another
As if the four horsemen area coming
Not to be a fiction of an angel
Just to become a human again, and live

Tafamo

Slowly, daily, and softly
She loves and moves
They gaze, she notions
Yet I don't fit in, I try

Gentle, fingertips, I'm in
Imploding, trying not to scare
Unable to hold back, I'm lost
Her eyes, her smile, lucky me

Amazed, by grace, hers only
Quiet in nature, nurturing
I come to you for air, shared air
At her side, I feel lucky

Where Will You Be

When the sun comes up and you remember me, as you hear the rain begin to fall and your gut tells you "perhaps he was it".
When you ask your friends about me, and they all say, you screwed up.
And you can't hold your head high.
Sure, you looked nice, very well put together, but why so much emphasis on what will one day be nothing but a memory.
I did not push you to any limit for you to treat me this way, but that's fine. I will put up with it, after all, I promised I would.
Where will you be as the sun flies across the sky and it finally hits you, how good I treated you, how much I put up with.
Forgive me if I sound bitter, as it is not my intent.
But if through my eyes you were to see.
Perhaps then you'd also ask yourself, where will you be.

In Hopes of One Day Left

I must be patient
Remain true to my words
As turmoil takes flight
And I sit like a potted plant
Will it all be okay?
I know it so, they do too
To leave in pitch black
Racing days on the end
This spine in pain, twisted
My eyes still shot red
All of it, all just fine
A smile painted on my face
In hope of just one more day.

Rush; Deep Impact

As we loved mutually
From dawn to dusk
The depth of your words
My shallow ones
Is it my fault?

I am but one being
Each diastolic beat
The marks of our war
He has forgotten us, it seems

Why must it be?
As the procreation failed
Tears for a black hole
Those freckles upon your face

Such strength at hand
Feel it once, twice, and more?
It became a rush
Amusement for you

My light went dim
No burden for you
Am I not dead?
I love you.

Six Hours Apart

The sun sets and rises
Bodies cold and alone
Thoughts cross oceans
And the will to be remains

The coals turned to ashes
As the story was told
Volcanoes erupted
And the sky was gray

So it rained misery
Look! In the distance
That star shines through
With piercing light and warmth

Another journey begins
With eyes staring
One at a time, longing
The big hand rules, it's time.

Not True, But First

They will tell you
Sometimes show you
Mostly convince you
Yet it's nowhere near
It has been won.

Not all who won could win
Mostly loss for a cause
Not yet grown
But ready to die
Not by bullet, by oath
Yet it was won

Empty rooms, lost sons
Still, beating and breathless
Already on a journey
The dust awaits
As family does too
Yet it was won

All gone, no more stardom
The invincibility cloak
Shredded, unrecoverable
Now, tubes and pipes
A machine of life, dying alive
Yet it was won

Walked further down the line
Time, endlessly slow and fast
Marked and scarred
Those back, now tightly knit
By burn, sounds and hardship
Yet is was... Maybe

To the Lost

The insanity remains, I fume, I am mad
Of all the harvested hate some seem to have.

Here at home, it roots at the highest tip
The suits, disconnected from us, not giving a shit.

Mourning continues, although I hope not again
History will just repeat what it did back when.

Regulation and change do not fit their personal plan
Neither left nor right, but of these facts I am no fan!

More lives to be lost, unfortunate but true
Don't ask what is done, but what you can do.

Reject the idea of hate as it just leads to dismay
Allow in your heart and mind for love a place to stay

Alive: I

Covered in fear
Cowering in a corner
Yet, with the will to live
Slowly rising as a fire does
And the feathers of crows fall
Covering the sky in black
Denying the sun access to life
And the clouds in anger cry
And the plants begin to wither
And the frost and snow
Steal every color
In preparation
To die.

Poor Man's Choice

My world stood up well together
The sun would wake me like a bullet of faith
Days, weeks, and months… The ideals evolved
"I will never, I know better, I will never"
Words that resonated through my mind
Unrelenting smiles, because of you
In a professional manner, always stayed on track
Walking, speaking, and being safe
An assortment on acquaintances as well as friends
I did not belong to a circle but my own
Two words, "try this" I say "no", just one "hit"
Slip, fall, stumble and tumble… On and on
Darkness descends, no eye to my hurricane
Paper-thin walls of life begin to rip apart
The once lit flame is now wailing, begging to survive
It was made, a single choice, endless damage
Years pass, society to blame, perhaps not
I own all these, these shreds of garments
Mother Nature is unforgiving, a lesson to learn
Starlit roof, a song composed by tires
Long I search, inside and out, up and down
It beats, with a melody of hope, an opportunity
Start again, not from the start, where I left off
The pursuits of happiness begun a second ago

Jack of all Trades

Some hearts can't
Even when they try
Some hearts won't
So, they begin to cry

It hurts to start
But also, to end
Wanting to be part
Not knowing when

Trapped within the trade
Endless flavor and scent
Pupils easily swayed
Not to listen while bent

Clubs, hearts, and a smile
A button, pompadour, and cuff
Desiring one, a small while
Unknowing just how tough

Exterior arms wide open
With a smile so fun
A promise, all broken
With a smile like the sun

In darkened rooms, four feet
With a bouncing motion
Not knowing what is defeat
Just a reciprocal notion

On a Void

As if returned to sender
Perhaps the wrong address
Maybe the contents are wrong
You did not order this
Did you?
The wrapping, in leaves and fall
Poetry atop a boulder
And you ran away in darkness
Yet it was too late
A seed, a thought, and a smile

Hundred Percent

Not two but one
Most often with none

Stray, lost in need
Of affections seed

Uphill, hard battles
My heart rattles

The keys you hold
Let me out in the cold

Give you the powers
Most days hours

Emotional distress
You don't see this mess

Is it time to have fun?
Maybe time to run

Please have no fear
Will always be here

Half Life

Perhaps it is true
More than once alive
Much more than few
The times I survive

Sometimes with regrets
Some days glazed with joy
Received without frets
Some days that destroy

Alive: II

A renaissance
Through a simple act
As the sun again smiles
Bringing youth, a key element
And colors radiate as soaring birds
Covering the sky in light
Giving way to a dire need again
As the wind whistles happily
songs through branches
the life of the dead
Has returned
Yet again
To live.

Ashes Left Behind

As canonized names were given sanctity
Blood and miracles for them, all together
Through the oceans and the storms
In names of kings, dukes, and queens

Thankful for all who give, mother earth first
Boar and fish, fire and rain, sacrifices made
Come to life, to suffer in its pains
Die to enter another journey

Forth then, centuries on after
Remains, reminders in the foliage
Lost steps and cities gone
Dialects that slowly fade

Gods then, from the earth itself
Fulfilling all promises, staying in the skies
One's life is worth all lives
Given blood to quench the thirst

Tragedy! Oh, tragedy slowly comes
Bearing colors, ever distant from home
Leaving all behind, unplanned mistake
Bringing misery, ideals, and imposed destiny

Forth then, sunrise and sunset, over and over
All which was left lingers still
Homage is paid to the end, no more blood
At journey's start, pay with closed eyes

Now then elsewhere, careless
Lack of honor by naive, yet insulting
See back through millennia
Real eyes, realize it's not yours

Bad Thoughts

Never felt as if there was enough of me
I failed, I failed to see with others' eyes
Only outward, where my focus was lost
Yet you came to me, and I to you.
Through time and space, and time again
I failed and punished those around me
You gave me heaven, with all your heart
And I carelessly only returned hell
I saw rivers on your face
They flowed so often, so powerful
I let the levees of my pride hold strong
Scared of being drowned in so much love
While also scared of loving back
Seeing your smile made dark days bright
Feeling you near me, it was blissful
The traces of these demons, lurked and hunted
Watching every move I made
Waiting like a stalking butler
They seeped through my most inner core
And only let me reap and sow misery

Emasculation: Through Kind Words

S As you suffered in silence
And sometimes out loud
Tears rolled down your cheeks
I saw your heart in a cloud

When I tried to make excuses
You wouldn't let me be
I tried to understand you
Yet it was too hard for me

I saw you hurt through the months
Not willing to listen or accept
That the Jekyll and Hyde
Was me, not giving you respect

And you yelled and screamed
Not with any malice at all
Just telling me to listen
To listen to you, once and for all

Now, we sit in crosshairs
I cried while we were apart
Dreading having been
That monster from the start

But let me make one thing clear
I will drown that Hyde, I vow
Let me show you that I can be
The best man that I know how

The Fall Around Me

When the leaves turn brown
And the free ones go south
While the rivers cry slowly
The blankets prepared
They begin to be bare
Fearless of judgements
Our tasteless complaints
If they too deserve it
A renaissance, soon
Just not now, not now
As eyes lift to the skies
Here they come, steady.

Cold Patch

Hide it as it may
These endless steps
That bring decay

Covered once again
By memories of pasts
So hard then to attain

These days and years
Adding up and slowly
Increasing endless fears

A voice of no reason
Speaking softly and aloud
The end of love's season

In the Contrasts

One looks lost and forgotten.
The other found, ever present.
Side by side, both ignored.
Yet so similar in heartbeats.

As liquor and family.
Sit as happy neighbors.
With two values so distant.
A promise from both.

The bricks are comfort to one.
A sunny, warm chain to the other.
So caring and so careless.
Where have we gone?

Forgiveness will be hard to get.
While in flesh, it'll hurt.
And none will walk alone.
As we are loved unconditionally

Step on the Stones Above the Water

Be not the person who you seek to find
Be the person who lives in your mind

Do not always admire or aspire life's wonder
For your thoughts are inside, go ahead...wander

Vacuity before and yet the same perhaps after
Point your nose forward, move onward with laughter

Fight if you must, if your motives are correct
The bigger burden will be, if you fail to protect

Those you value most and the values as they are
Follow them from start to end and you will go far

Believe in something, or naught as you may
Just bear in mind; without a god, you will go astray

Clutch the water, smell ocean through the air
Your mind despite its struggles, is still fair

Do not leave and say "I forgot to live"
For these foul words are a terrible present to give

Your eyes grow heavy, for it is a bit past eleven
Close them, thank god, and touch heaven.

Layers

At first sight, I knew, it was clear
That we'd found each other dear
Now sitting in quiet, as a child in fear
All I want is your words in my ear

Ironclad heart, stands no chance
When our eyes meet, within a quick glance
I lose my composure, crumbling my stance
I walk toward you, I advance

Coincidental, but 920 is not a time
But two hearts crossing a line
With my poetry, my words, sublime
I desperately fear feelings aren't fine

But it is worth it, I will admit
That perhaps quiet I should sit
Contemplate, reason a bit
A complex fight that summons not wit

Forgive me dear, if I'm inexact
If my emotions bring you to tear
Never will I, my words retract
I'm lovingly and endless yours dear

A Day of Do and Do

That such emotion has been quite ill
For in those days, it expressed its will.

Through those eyes that shone so bright
As if in their hearts laid an infinite light.

Special one, a day of smiles nonetheless
With vast worlds together in happiness

Those in between, and that him and her
Rejoice in that sanctity that is to share

Preach now that the universe agrees
On those events that one rarely foresees
As precious bonds are formed this day
With strangers' smiles that so much say

Not a feeling nor emotion left intact
Knowing well how to make a pact

Love has won the beat of your heart
The wish is that you'll never be apart

Shrug to Kismet

As it comes and goes
When it fails you
If you regret it
For a stolen kiss
Perhaps a bit more
It is yours, embrace it
As the flowers do the sun
And the earth does the water
Naturally and simply
With those tears
That touch your smile
Believe in my one truth
I may not tell it again
Hug me, for I may be
That meteorite rain
Your red beating planet
Needs for its renaissance
I will believe and trust in you
As I barely can in me
Count the countless seconds
You have suffered elsewhere
Now, close your eyes
Show that compassionate smirk
Feel these hands
With their simple job
To care, to show a world
Your habitat

Let your mind live
Your heart sing
And be
The true owner of it all
Yes?

Fill Less

Brisk and sudden on shorter days
Falling back, falling down
Derived from shades of brown
Painting the soil, inch by inch

Through the glass, sometimes
A feeling of warmth, breathing
Yet at times so much more
As they undressed in the cold

Some flee as if avoidable
Here they come, symmetrical
Minutes pass without return
No time to think of time

Times of desolation, death even
Uneven rays of sun, they too hide
As the canvases' vibrant colors die
With bare souls, patiently filled

Snaketh

Standing in the dark
With piercing eyes
Waiting for the fear
Waiting for the fret
The vexation that comes
As clouds of doubts
Obstruct the eyes, the soul

In patience, in death, in life
When salt and water fill
An ocean full of ships
And waves crash
The storm then settles
Finally, looking up
Some life remains

Those scales change
Another day to grow
The systolic and diastolic
A melody, always on beat
From beginning to end
The simplest of reminders
That one poisonous bite
Does not always kill

At Odds

On highchair, crossed feet
Listening to songs outside
Wondering if they sing for you
And those thoughts travel

Wondering if all fires will drown
And the whistle continues
Songs with endless echoes
And clouds can't sit still

Counting odds, in plain dark
Yet darkest hours come
All while you take steps
I hope toward me, I hope.

In Sight, yet not Always in Mind

When we tend to pass each other on by
Uncaring and free when times just die
Forgetting as well, we are never alone
Painting a canvas of home, your very own

A humble thought, a look, an idea
Of things that drive us to see what's clear
What we want and how we see it
Although unplanned, that same idea, so be it

The cross of stares, and our words exchange
Sharing past memories that seem so strange
Sitting in dark, with third party just there
Often, feeling so near, trading a glare

At last! Oh... So at last! Feeling what is soft
Only to give way, to what can be roughed
To only try this, and have one close to me
Leaving a trace, entangled in what could be

As sun rises and wind blows through and through
There laying, entangled, what more is there to do
In lack of sleep and no real will to begin the day
One would want for this feeling to just stay

Extremities that run through a dead cell
Making it seem these days will end well
But not today, now enclosed in both minds
Perhaps to come again together in nearer times?

This is and That is, More

Sitting up, looking at the silence
Listening, to that soft smirk
Melodic, ever so hypnotic, breathe
"The only peaceful time," such joke

Head and heart, both hurt, just a bit
Wines and spirits, now hit harder
Aching, perhaps it is age, or not
Push, one-step more, and push again

Dark, fire sparks flying, peace indeed
Memories of past, perhaps some to come
That soft smile, glowing eyes, star-struck
Ambivalent on words, just sometimes

Inching closer, you have let me in, perhaps
As clear as Sunday skies, burning imprints
Feeling what is endlessly free, careless
Learning, slowly, at the mercy of water

Writing then, a prologue for this book
Adventure and mystery on every page
Quiet times too have their edge
Recurring characters, far between

Habits changed, maybe for the better
Ever present, the present in mind
Wait for the rolling, pour then
To partake, sometimes also dark

Pundit artist, saying little with none
Rubbing slowly, fingers and hand
Allow this to be recurring, later
Chapters will pass before resuming

Struck Luck: 15

Not looking but finding
Wanting, at times needing
Fifteen months binding
Yet always lonely reading

Promises, so often broken
This heart never wandered
And you barely responded
Taken for granted loves token

Barely present, always far
Not knowing what to do
To be felt, perhaps seen too
Asking for little, then more

Words that are meaningless
Not without at least some action
Love, shown love, real interaction
Get rid of that cause of stress

Now with your smile to pretend
Days past, together don't exist
Like morning fog, mountains mist
Half turn to not hurt in the end

Such Depth of your Smile

The details which entail your leer
My! Oh my! Such is life, such is mine
Not in this existence yet, no, oh Lord we are
Sneeze in frigid cold November time.

The glass of the heart, abundant with love
Autonomous you, bashful at times, me
Graceful as the wind, perhaps you're from above
I can only scratch the surface that we see.

Vibrant as rainbow colors, your endearment to all
It makes me smile, this blue home we share
Spread your wings; shine ever so bright, your call

Leave a city, a bridge, the love of those who care
Anxious to assemble a new memory with you all
The contrast of our eyes, I feel the love filled stare.

Failure: the Absence of Success

So, why is it? Why is it I failed and feel absolutely mad?
That I've let people fail, I let people down.
Reality is; I blame no one, yet knowing so makes me sad
Reminisce that feeling of youth…that feeling when I drown.

A void, a black hole of the heart you may say
Trying some things the first time and going frigid
20 more until 29 and the feeling won't slip away
The road is easy here, yet it feels so rigid

Allow me to abscond or leave me to stay
Tomorrow to wake at dawn and knowing
Am I really made of what is needed? Who am I to say?

Scold me if you may, pasture of truth I'm mowing
I shall not fail tomorrow, although I did today
In the river of adversity, with audacity I'll keep rowing

Day In, Day Out

As I walk past you
And your smirk hides
Knowing well what you've done
Perhaps thinking, possibly
That my spirit would stray
Or I could be devastated

Oh, how wrong you are
As I was and will be
That same person, me
And this too will pass
This storm full of animosity
But it too will reach you

Yet your pride, so "gallant"
It too, will have to end
But not you, maybe yours
If you are indeed blessed
Will pay in dark days
What you've done in "rights"

Shoulder on Hand

Bare feet, light stretch
Seeking for a possible contest
Layer... Wipe, talk and layer again
Not this way, this way feels like home
Look up, move and feel the aches, stubborn
Feel that, almost a second layer of roots
Time stops, breathing slackens, hands quiver
Now, the force escapes through every pore
Fingers fighting against high gravity
Transferring all this strength
Nearly there, so close
Last move, there!

Round two
Similar rituals, reverse roles
Gracious, smirking while pondering
Failing to follow any advice, for the thrill
However, put in best context a "be careful"
Loading, one, two, three and four. Skillful
Layer once, look at the binding, ready to conquer
One last look, now the dance starts
Every step, sometimes pain, strong
A waltz, ascending, such moves
Gazing up to be alert
Done, float down

Touch

The skies with those eyes
Earth with your feet
The oceans with your heart
Leave behind you a trail of joy
As only you know how
Be the change you wish to see
Continue to go far
From the routines go astray
Your heart knows the way
Share this planet
Be gentle with others
All the places you get to see
Take a mental photograph
Save that moment
Frozen in time
For the rest of your life
Take the risks that many don't
Live and love living
Touch the horizons of the world

Facing Capsize

Those waves, only known when grown
Peaceful as a breeze, sometimes deadly
A port saw a ship float away, carelessly
Lives seen, pains felt, and yet it floats

For some time with aim, more often not
Encountering the resistance of the world
However, all the names remembered
All alive and waiting for their turn

Tough times, so abundantly still
As the sway, back and forth, is sickening
All part of the treasure of life
Sometimes a wish to see land

A current ongoing battle, tested, yet again
Sails true to its strength, slowly navigating
Those hurt, believe the mighty tales
That ship belongs always at sea, alone

Sweet Words

That you speak
And I cautiously hear
Oh dearest darling!
When you are near

Three, sometimes more
Heavenly unmistakable
Your smile and eyes
So impossible to ignore

Fell my languid fingers
Seek your heart beat
When you exhale quietly
And each breath lingers

Say the words, you know how
We have not met
So these are the words
I can say to you now.

Mariana Eyes

Walking simply, light hearted
Seems from afar, it started
While I got closer I could see
And feel something inside of me

A vibration, reverberating in my soul
Consuming me as I stood whole
Each sense in shock! Or more so ecstasy
How could this happen, how could this be?

Inching closer, these waters feel so cold
The same cold feeling, now feels so old
Half a turn, a smile, and those eyes
Welcoming and charming, no surprise!

Teach me a thing or two, perhaps more
I'll also share with you what I adore
And how they've made me feel grown
Stories and trips of places gone

Time passes, at times too fast
But until now, we've made it last
Continue indulging me in your sea
I will not lose myself, I'll let things be

A Lone Stride to Fall

The winds of winter have come and gone.
Reciprocated smiles, at times innocent
Damage to a soul that is sensitive and prone
In a simple life, most maladies are easy to prevent

Three lights that shine forth from deep inside
Emaciated hairline, yet it retains its natural splendor
Smile here, giggle there, legitimate strength, heart of pride
Hidden from plain view. Oh! but there is much more

Create a new photographable memory day by day
Live to be happy, live to enjoy life's beauty
Close your eyes and allow yourself to go astray
Walk barefoot as if it is your sole duty

Slide your slender fingers on the water
Your eyes closed, learn with your heart to see
The three hundred and sixty-five days do not matter
Every breath and every beat, for you to be

Wear your favorite shirt, always match your smile
Stay around, let your presence be a present
With your blue eyes look up, match the sky for a while
You! Yes, quite unique ever so pleasant

Unequivocal Love

I'm in a daze
My head's a craze
When I see you
And I'm near you

I love the pieces
This love our thesis
I see you, a blink
You smirk, a wink

Love me now then
And tell me when
When you're ready for me
So, we a family can be

Beautiful Star Dust

I saw you come home
With smiles and closed eyes
The breathing, gentle as a breeze
Not a word, with soft tugs

Those steps, joy!
That first kick—mio figlio/mia figlia
That glass you broke, pulled off the table
Those puzzles, your love

Few words, one of many "Forza"
And I love you endlessly
Flesh of my flesh
Blood of my blood

That first prime birthday
It would be quite a party
All the oddities you'd love
I see you, as if there

Yet, none can come true
And I sit wondering
What you'd love
Maybe tomatoes?

I hope you're flying, that you see me
That you feel my love
Because I can't feel you
As you never were here.

Double Sunrise

The sands were still
Cool with every layer
Each layer a stroke
With an endless paint

Drowned and gone
homes made, and broken
Sidestepping at high tide
Those endless grains, foes

Not their home
But there still, again
Depart soon, be gone
Darkness, friend here.

A Certain Hour

Not certain I found you or if you found me.
All I know is, it made me happy as can be.
Your simple smile, was all could and wanted to see.

Those life lines that met, was it coincidence?
Just seeing you, in light and dark made me feel so intense.
Not a day has gone by, when I don't love your presence.

You're goddess, queen, the most precious gem I call.
I make mistakes, sorry, I'll do my best to not let you fall.
With all my being, I want and will give you one thing, all!

Genuine Care

It is hard to find and harder to keep
One of those qualities
That you endlessly and carefully seek

Often confused and at times tossed around
Sold for gold and silver to the lost
Whose life's meaning is not yet found

See the world through other troubled eyes
Do not be blinded by the illusion
Worldly specters created in disguise

The option of holding back we contend
Why hide your truest essence?
Knowing well, we go home at the end

Be forgiving to those far and near
Listen to the docile thoughts
Which will rid you of such fear

Feel the warmth of someone's hand
When love is manifested
The world you've changed, will take a stand

Nothing, is Okay

Conjured up from nothing seen
Nothing tangible at all
Once feelings that were keen
Perhaps inner fear of the fall

Tears and screaming, sad joys
Start to learn what is to be
All the madness, all the toys
Blood should run, and run with glee

In four, two or three, maybe none
Seeing nothing most of days
Traces and marks, all to be gone
Incinerated, blown away with sun rays

Endless search, nothing found
At first scream and last breath
Nothing matters, not a sound
In the end, awaiting death

Antigua in Pax (la receta)

There, a cobblestone, stories
The children's sounds
Coffee, street scents and food
A brisk valley breeze, cold
And that one looking downward
Incessantly and ever beautiful
Finding refuge in a time capsule
Disguised as the quietest of rooms
The morning view, the bet
Of a million to one, to be there
Being present and breathing
Irreplaceable, not the first time
Perhaps not the last either
And in between some discourse
Rose from within, the sense
That which allowed for smiles
And so, forth the footprints double
Before the next day begins

An Intuitive Existence in the Rest of the World

The key is to be keen
Life will give you maladies
Allow yourself to mourn
Enjoy life's joy the same
Cross your fingers with hope
See the foliage revive at dawn
Speak daily to god
Whoever he may be
The infinite plan for life
Be a part of it
You are not a mere person
Catch your breath over and over
Look to the horizon
Take a stance and dive firmly
Live the rest of your life

I Almost Gave Up

When I saw you there
Laying on the ground
As my heart beat irregularly

When my eyes could see no evil
None from you at least
As my bare feet felt the cold dirt

When your words seemed to fade
I almost gave up
It seemed logical, well somewhat

When those fingers tried to reach
Without strength to do so
And your voice remained so gentle

When I reminisced about those days
Filled with seemingly endless tears
Due in part to your and my fears

When words weren't enough
To take back the damage done
So irreparable, so much of it

When you turned your back and left
As you knew my weakness
I could say nothing

When it was me who was dying
I woke up and smiled, with you by my side
As I knew, I'll never give up on you.

As if

The clouds could form a life
Or I could be born again
Or perhaps it is not that simple
To forge frontiers of a true self
When selfless is the only lit way

Those tears and term we live for
Knowing that the rope will end
For love and fear of loss
A human touch is what we need
Maybe in form of a kiss, or not

Leaning against a pale March
While February never came
And the beats we heard not
The imprint forever will lay
And I'll forever say, I love you

One Face Coin

Spins and twirls, cutting through the air
Spitting plural words, trying to be fair
Unbeknown to all, who simply fall
And simply see the spin, unwilling to call

Always the choice, untold
The wait, letting actions unfold
A sense of help, and superior
Hiding the other side's interior

Perhaps the forging made those ridges
Crossing since, and burning bridges
While flipping with charm and allure
Building then, ways to keep ships ashore

Fretfully, a choice is made, before it all
Waiting, pondering, wishing for a fall
Yet there is nothing but the spin
Seeing the side, call it mid-air, and win.

Finding You Within a Mirror

Maybe now it was me
Perhaps just my turn
Time and space crash
Fear blue and red flashes
Everything but guilty
A color made me run
That was enough to cuff

No more a name or a smile
Another number in a block
Suits, robe abs, and Glocks
Born in a wrong era, not color
No longer a hunter or king
Hung by twelve, diverse
Each a bias of its own

As many wrinkles as years
Many friends, stories, replica
Letters, saviors of sanity
Seeds left turned to trees
Cannot reap its fruits
Trying one more time
Too much to bear, freedom

Irreplaceable

Swimming before I was here
Through my mother's every breath
As you fall and give me joy
When you sing those melodies

Going with me everywhere
Coming back the same way
Joyous moments with those friends
Making memories that don't fade

While gazing through a window
Often breaking nights quietness
With drops drawing short paths
Quenching thirst in every corner

Most of me, most of us, all around
Purest essence of life itself
As you always do, smile again
Thank you dearest, water.

Accent

With a twang so slight
The word escapes
With rocks in sight
And plastic drapes

All heard, stories of the heart
The coming's not near
Pondering the hard start
Luckily, skies are clear

A voice that said aloud
One-way ticket, to Texas I'll go
Nearby a trivial crowd
A thought, it's funny, no?

Another Drop of Rum

Give without expecting back, just give
Another drop of rum
To forget the maladies, maybe for a while

To help those feelings retrieve
Another drop of rum
Drink some more, drink in style

That bottle, those life friends
Another drop of rum
Sun that sets and with majesty rises

All of it, as it begins, it has to, it ends
Another drop of rum
Be scared not, rejoice in surprises

Sing as loud as you want and can
Another drop of rum
Redefine your priorities on earth

In life and beyond, make a stand
Another drop of rum
You are loved from birth until death

Truck or Van

A morning breath
Speak to new friends
With old tongues
To remember where's home

Layers, not too many
They may be peeled
Breaths and fumes
Motors warming up

Flashing lights, sirens distant
Fearless, home awaits so far
Resourceful yet wasteful
Backbone to these homes

Minimalists so rich
Rules written by greed
Unapplied equally
Yet there is some accord

Unspoken unless spoken
Translations can be dead
Nails and screws
Learning to not starve

Too hot, too cold, snow!
Matters not, slave still
Feed with fear, going home
Laying, food is death

Think not of one
Trip was worth it
Multiples are enough
Longing to go back

Ever so Bright

On random days, the coffee is made for two
In case one morning, both skins touch again—
While counting stars and sheep, in hopes of sleep
As the heat rises, while it longs for that presence
Fingers searching for that smile—absent
The night feels endless, the room feels cold
A single thought and a single line—
Whispering that name, as if shouting for it
This linear way, moving the hands, tirelessly
And of all dark places, of all sounds and feelings
With all the abyss and unknown
There is just one, one celestial body
Enfolding all that once was, yet so pure
Light then, the days to come!

Feeling in Silence

At times, I feel in silence, I sit there still
At times, I lose hope and all my will

There are days when words do not suffice
And their lack of, is cold, cold as ice

I remember the days when walking alone
And to find you, made the feeling unknown

I thought that I was dreaming while I awake
With your grace, and smiles, a treat to take

Now that stamp of your smile leaves me with a scent
It makes me smirk, yet I don't know where it went

My heart has no regrets, knowing you is my win
Now and then, I feel you near, and I can't help but grin

Unnecessary are the modest words, as I still see your eyes
Sitting still in your corner, and me in mine as time flies

Doubtless: Preamble to a Story

Not a single doubt or mistake
A second look I had to take

To see then what is now clear
That I wanted you, close and near

Through the crowds and the ropes
I then lost my words and found hope

Seeing this as perhaps a collision
Maybe two of us, lost on our mission

The looming deadline, sat atop
Embedded mutually in minds, can't stop

Feelings of numbness take over and hum
With your smile, no longer feeling numb

The depth of those eyes, and light of your smile
Only inside I blush, while I glare at you awhile

All the new challenges and emotions
Feeling assured and so secure, not simple notions

Through hardships and city's time
A mutual emotion, standing on each other's line

On some directions now, words begin to fly
Scribbles and mistakes, for you I will try

The beauty and magic of words before
Patience on all ends to receive more

Now here with you, hold me near
And I will whisper, thank you dear

In full awe, I can only hope upon this hillside
That you are happy with me by your side

Amongst All

So many faces, so very many.
All dull, why? Life is going by.
Radiant, you stood there.

I, hiding beneath my dark hair.
Unable to fit with such crowd.
You, such an unconventional element.

Narrow stairs, escalating thoughts.
Unparalleled & sublime beauty.
Beating, slowly to revive... A heart

Again today, as countless other days.
We face our deep dark eyes.
Uncertain, unsure of what we want.

The night is ours, of that I'm certain
You look absolutely amazing.
This old town will be painted with smiles.

Give me today a kiss again.
Put me on the cloud that you lay in.
Lucky sun that shone on you.

Analogous to China's are your walls.
I cannot give up, I heed too much to quit.
Show and tell, show and tell.

Between some, we live and exist.
We both suffer from the fear.
Among some and among all.

www.ingramcontent.com/pod-product-compliance
Lightning Source LLC
Chambersburg PA
CBHW032050040426
42449CB00007B/1057